LIGHTNING BOLT BOOKS™

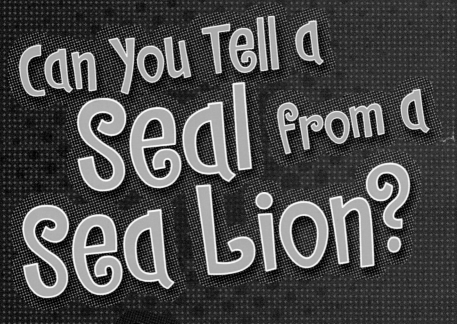

Can You Tell a Seal from a Sea Lion?

Buffy Silverman

Lerner Publications Company
Minneapolis

Lerner Publications Company
A division of Lerner Publishing Group, Inc.
241 First Avenue North
Minneapolis, MN 55401 U.S.A.

Website address: www.lernerbooks.com

Library of Congress Cataloging-in-Publication Data

Silverman, Buffy.
    Can you tell a seal from a sea lion? / by Buffy Silverman.
        p.   cm. — (Lightning bolt books.™ — Animal look-alikes)
    Includes index.
    ISBN 978-0-7613-6738-3 (lib. bdg : alk. paper)
    1. Seals (Animals)—Juvenile literature. 2. Sea lions—Juvenile literature. I. Title.
QL737.P6S48 2012
    599.79—dc23   2011028974

Manufactured in the United States of America
1 — CG — 12/31/11

Table of Contents

Ear Flaps or Ear Holes?

Seals and sea lions look a lot alike. They have flippers instead of front and back feet. They swim with their flippers.

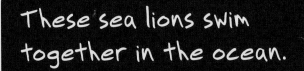

These sea lions swim together in the ocean.

Both seals and sea lions are mammals. Like all mammals, they drink their mothers' milk when they are babies. Mammals also have hair. Do you see this seal's fur?

This young harp seal is very furry. Older seals and sea lions aren't as furry, but they do have some hatir on their bodies.

Mammals breathe air.

Seals and sea lions hold their breath underwater. They dive and catch fish. Then they both swim up to the surface to gulp fresh air.

This seal swims near the surface of the water as it breathes.

But you can tell these animals apart. Look at this sea lion's head. An ear flap sticks out from each side. Sea lions hear better underwater than on land.

Sea lions listen to the barks of other sea lions when they are on land.

Seals have no ear flaps. But they do have ears! A small opening on each side of the head leads to their ears. They listen to find food and to stay safe.

A hole on the side of a seal's head leads to its ear.

This seal's whiskers help it find fish.

Seals and sea lions use their whiskers to feel moving water. Moving water tells them that fish are near.

Front and Back Flippers

A seal pushes through water with its big back flippers. Its back flippers spread apart like fans. They wave from side to side.t

A sea lion
paddles
with its front
flippers. The
front flippers are
long and strong.
Each front flipper
has short nails and
no hair.

A seal steers underwater with its small front flippers. The front flippers have fur. Look at the long claws on this seal's front flippers. It scratches with its claws.

A sea lion steers underwater with its back flippers. They are shorter than its front flippers.

The sea lion moves its back flippers to turn underwater.

Sea lions turn their back flippers underneath their bodies to move on land. They scoot across rocks and sand on four flippers.

A seal cannot tuck its back flippers under its body. It slides and rolls on its belly. It looks like a caterpillar when it slides forward. But some seals can move fast on land. Some move faster than people!

On Land

Seals and sea lions often leave the water. They gather on rocks, sand, or ice. This is called hauling out. Sea lions use their front flippers to pull themselves out of the water.

This sea lion has pulled itself out of the water using its flippers.

Seals use the tide to reach rocks and beaches. They swim ashore when the tide is high. Then they wriggle out of the water.

A harbor seal made it onto this rock when the tide was high.

Seals and sea lions haul out to rest and to shed their fur.

They also give birth on land.

A baby seal stays close to its mother.

Hundreds of sea lions gather in groups. The groups are called colonies. Sea lions bark, roar, and grunt in their colonies.

Some seals don't like a crowd. Harbor seals swim alone. They spread apart when they haul out on beaches. Usually, they are quiet. A harbor seal growls and snorts if another seal touches it.

A male sea lion defends his place on land. His barks and roars tell other males to stay away. Male sea lions grow more than twice as large as female sea lions.

Male and female harp seals gather on ice. A male may blow bubbles and make noises below the ice to get a female's attention. Male harp seals are only a little larger than the females.

A group of harp seals lay and slide on snowy ice.

Growing Up

Baby seals and sea lions are called pups. A pup drinks its mother's milk. The milk has lots of fat. The pup grows quickly.

This baby sea lion drinks milk from its mother.

A pup grows a thick layer of fat under its skin. The fat is called blubber. Blubber keeps seals and sea lions warm in cold water.

This baby seal has developed a layer of fat to keep warm in icy water.

A harp seal pup has white fur. It makes the pup hard to see on ice. A mother harp seal feeds her pup for ten to twelve days. Then she leaves. The pup swims and catches fish on its own.

A mother harp seal pokes her head out of the ice and greets her pup.

A California sea lion pup knows its mother's call. It bleats when it hears its mother. The pup stays with its mother for about one year.

Seals and sea lions swim in oceans. They haul out on beaches and rocks. Can you tell these look-alikes apart?

Who Am I?

Look at the pictures below. Which ones are seals? Which ones are sea lions?

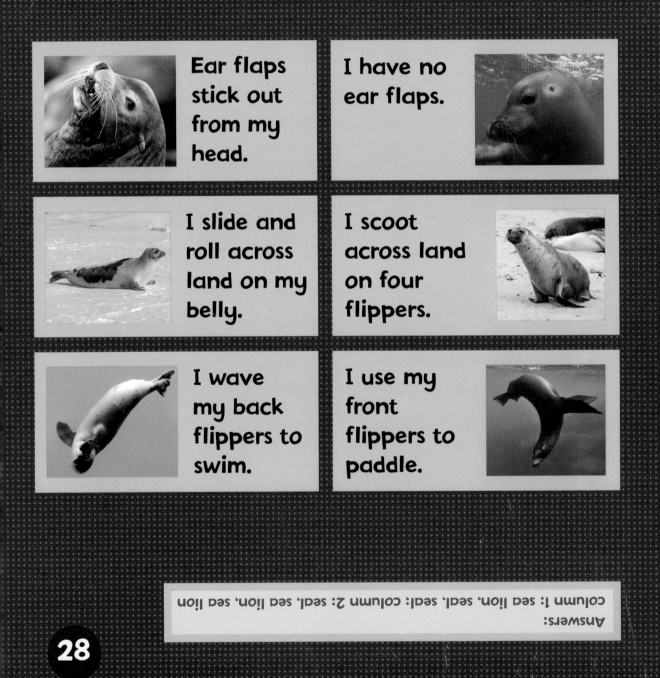

Ear flaps stick out from my head.

I have no ear flaps.

I slide and roll across land on my belly.

I scoot across land on four flippers.

I wave my back flippers to swim.

I use my front flippers to paddle.

Fun Facts

- Gray seals sleep underwater. Without waking, they come to the surface to breathe.

- A hooded seal pup drinks its mother's milk for only five to twelve days. The pup doubles its weight in that time.

- Male sea lions roar like lions. And some male sea lions have fur around their necks as lions do.

- Fur seals are more closely related to sea lions than to other seals. Fur seals have ear flaps. And they walk on four flippers.

- A Weddell seal can stay underwater for more than an hour. It dives 2,000 feet (600 meters) below the surface.

Glossary

bleat: to cry out.
Calves, sheep, and sea lion pups bleat.

blubber: a thick layer of fat under an animal's skin

colony: a group of animals of the same kind living together

flipper: a wide, flat limb that is used for swimming

haul out: to climb out of the water onto land

mammal: a group of animals that breathes air, has hair, and drinks their mother's milk

shed: to lose or drop fur

tide: the regular rise and fall of sea levels due to the pull of the moon's gravity

whiskers: the long hairs growing near the mouth of an animal

Further Reading

Alaska Fisheries Science Center: What Marine Mammals Eat
http://access.afsc.noaa.gov/MultimediaGallery/
details.php?gal=Videos%20only&rec=1052

Creature Features: Harp Seals
http://kids.nationalgeographic.com/kids/animals/
creaturefeature/harp-seals

Harvey, Jeanne Walker. *Astro: The Stellar Sea Lion.* Mount Pleasant, SC: Sylvan Dell Publishing, 2010.

Kalman, Bobbie, and John Crossingham. *Seals and Sea Lions.* New York: Crabtree Publishing, 2006.

Martin-James, Kathleen. *Harp Seals.* Minneapolis: Lerner Publications Company, 2009.

Ocean Living for Kids
http://nationalzoo.si.edu/Animals/OceanLiving/
ForKids/default.cfm

Index

Photo Acknowledgments

The images in this book are used with the permission of: © Loisik/Dreamstime.com, p. 1 (top); © Michael Zysman/Dreamstime, p. 1 (bottom); © Tui De Roy/Minden Pictures, pp. 2, 27 (bottom); © NHPA/SuperStock, p. 4; © Dale Wilson/All Canada Photos/Getty Images, p. 5; © James Hager/Robert Harding World Imagery/Getty Images, p. 6; © Glenn Nagel/Dreamstime.com, pp. 7, 28 (top left); © Hiroya Minakuchi/Minden Pictures, pp. 8, 28 (top right); © David Hecker/AFP/Getty Images, pp. 9, 28 (bottom left); © Brian J. Skerry/National Geographic/Getty Images, p. 10; © Andy Rouse/The Image Bank/Getty Images, pp. 11, 28 (bottom right); © David W. Middleton/SuperStock, p. 12; © James Morgan/Robert Harding World Imagery/Getty Images, p. 13; © Rozenn Leard/Dreamstime.com, pp. 14, 28 (middle right); © G. Carleton Ray/Photo Researchers, Inc., p. 15; © Gerald & Buff Corsi/Visuals Unlimited, Inc., pp. 16, 21; © Barnabas Kindersley/Dorling Kindersley/Getty Images, p. 17; © Roger Powell/naturepl.com, p. 18; © Tim Fitzharris/Minden Pictures, p. 19; © Paul Souders/Stone/Getty Images, p. 20; © Francois Gohier/Photo Researchers, Inc., pp. 22, 28 (middle left); © E. R. Degginger/Photo Researchers, Inc., p. 23; © Doug Allan/npl/Minden Pictures, p. 24; © Tom Brakefield/Brand X Pictures/Getty Images, p. 25; © age fotostock/SuperStock, p. 26; © James Urbach/SuperStock, p. 27 (top); © Martin Harvey/Gallo Images/Getty Images, p. 29; © Suzi Eszterhas/Minden Pictures, p. 30; © Photowitch/Dreamstime.com, p. 31.

Front cover: © Frank Greenaway/Dorling Kindersley/Getty Images (top); © Richard Lindie/Dreamstime.com (bottom).

Main body text set in Johann Light 30/36.